TORAH PORTIONS NOTEBOOK
מחברת פרשת

CREATED BY JOHN DIFFENDERFER

Torah Portions Notebook

Copyright © 2019 by John Diffenderfer. All rights reserved.

No part of this publication may be used, transmitted, copied, or reproduced without written permission of the author/publisher except in brief excerpts.

Quantity discounts are available on bulk purchases of this book for congregational, resale, educational, fundraising, or event purposes. For more information, visit JohnDiff.com.

ISBN: 978-0-692-03665-5
Printed in the United States of America.

ABOUT THE TORAH PORTIONS

The *Parashat HaShavua* (literally "portion of the week") comes from a Jewish tradition that began in the 6th century BCE. The practice of collective, weekly readings of the Torah is believed to have been birthed from the scribe Ezra's desire to see the Israelites remember and keep the Torah. In the Book of Nehemiah, we find the origin of this corporate study and the establishment of what today is commonly referred to as the "Torah Portions."

The traditional delineation of the various *parashot* (Hebrew plural for "portions") is found in the Torah scrolls from Ashkenazic, Sephardic, and Yemenite Jewish communities. There is ample historic evidence of their practice throughout both first centuries (BCE and CE) and continuing throughout the present day. Today, this traditional method of study remains widely used by both Jewish and Christian communities around the world.

Each Torah portion is tied to a specific week of the Jewish calendar. There are 54 portions in all. Depending on each Jewish year's length and how the religious holidays fall, the portions are read sequentially but may be interrupted by various holiday-specific readings. As such, several of the portions are traditionally combined to keep the reader on an annual schedule.

In this notebook, the dates are empty, so that they may be filled by you. This allows the book to remain timeless, regardless of the Gregorian or Jewish calendars' overlap or leap years. Additionally, the portions that are often combined to accommodate religious holidays have been indicated in the headings of their respective sections.

There is no limit to the depths of the Torah. Students of the Torah find meaning in every character, story, commandment, word, and letter of the original Hebrew text. This notebook is designed as a place for you to collect, organize, and preserve your findings. It's purposefully open-ended and draws the student through thoughtful analysis and personal application.

HOW TO USE THIS NOTEBOOK

This book is designed to be used on a weekly basis, according to the weekly Parashah (from the annual cycle for reading the Torah). Each heading shows the Scripture and titles, in both Hebrew and English, while allowing you to note your own dates and weeks.

Write the dates and Hebrew name. (See final page for Hebrew guide.)

DATE: October 26	WEEK: One

B'REISHEET, GENESIS 1:1-6:8
B'REISHEET, IN THE BEGINNING

בראשית

ב ר א ש י ת
Bet Resh Aleph Shin Yod Tav

List central info and events (i.e. "who did what.")

HEADLINES
1. The universe is created
2. Adam and Eve sin
3. Cain kills his brother Abel

Identify the thematic conflicts and narrative changes. Then, extrapolate morals and messages presented.

CONFLICT/CHANGE	LESSON/APPLICATION
Adam vs. Loneliness: He wants more than just Divine relationship	People are created for relationships: "Not good to be alone"
Eve is tricked by the half-truths of the Serpent	Sometimes, we can be deluded by things that seem to be true
Adam vs. Eve: United in sin, but turn against one another when confronted with shame and guilt.	- Fear destroys relationships. - Dishonesty is often rooted in shame. - Self-preservation kills relationships.
Cain kills Abel	Consequences echo throughout all generations.

Research and list words that hold deeper meaning.

KEYWORDS	DEFINITIONS
1. Adam	Mankind, Man, Humanity, etc. (Symbolic or Literal?)
2. Eve	Mother, Woman, Womankind…
3. Rib	Literally: "Side"
4. Good	Hebrew: Tov — Good, Complete, Final
5. Offering	Gift/tribute

Consolidate personally relevant revelation.

PERSONAL TAKEAWAYS
1. Everything comes from one source
2. Be on guard; The opportunity for sin is always present (as even in Eden)
3. Sin always disrupts shalom/community + causes separation/isolation

Reference Bible verses and other sources.

Use the main field to record general thoughts and findings. Add section breaks as desired. The nested bullet guides keep your notes clearly outlined.

REFERENCE	NOTES	
Gen. 1:1	• First introduced as "Creator".	F
	• When we create, we are engaging in divine practice	
	• Productivity is holy	B
Gen. 1: 6-8	• First mention of separation (heaven and earth)	F
	• Monday: The only day that wasn't called "good" ⚈	C
Gen. 2:18-23	• Eve created	F
	• Taken from the "side" of Adam/mankind	
	• Possible reference to mankind being unified before the division between male and female	
vs. 20	• Eve made to be "helper opposite" to Adam	P
	• Becomes source of future life	P
Gen. 2:24	• Children made to "leave father and mother"	P
Gen. 3	THE FALL	C
	• Serpent used desire for more power	
	• Adam didn't question Eve at first	
	• Was Eve ever told not to eat the fruit?	?
	• Was her "sin" from eating?	?
	• Or from giving Adam something HE was not supposed to eat?	?
r. Melton	• "Naked" = Same word used to describe the serpent's "craftiness/cunning"	X
	• Became like the serpent	C
	• Not "like G-d"	
Gen. 4	• Abel brought "firstlings" (firstfruits) of his flock	F
	• No mention of quality of Cain's offering	
	• Mincha offering (not for guilt/sin)	F
Lev. 2	• Later codified (also Ex. 29; 30; 40)	X

KEY   P: PROPHETIC   B: BLESSING   C: CURSE   F: FIRST OCCURRENCE   ?: QUESTION   X: CROSS REFERENCE

Categorize your notes based on common themes. Use the Key or add your own symbols.

DATE: WEK:

B'REISHEET, GENESIS 1:1-6:8
B'REISHEET, IN THE BEGINNING

Tav   Yod   Shin   Aleph   Resh   Bet

HEADLINES

1.
2.
3.

CONFLICT/CHANGE	LESSON/APPLICATION

KEYWORDS	DEFINITIONS
1.	
2.	
3.	
4.	
5.	

PERSONAL TAKEAWAYS

1.
2.
3.

REFERENCE	NOTES
	○ ○ ○
	○ ○ ○
	○ ○ ○
	○ ○ ○
	○ ○ ○
	○ ○ ○
	○ ○ ○
	○ ○ ○
	○ ○ ○
	○ ○ ○
	○ ○ ○
	○ ○ ○
	○ ○ ○
	○ ○ ○
	○ ○ ○
	○ ○ ○
	○ ○ ○
	○ ○ ○
	○ ○ ○
	○ ○ ○
	○ ○ ○
	○ ○ ○
	○ ○ ○
	○ ○ ○
	○ ○ ○
	○ ○ ○
	○ ○ ○
	○ ○ ○
	○ ○ ○
	○ ○ ○
	○ ○ ○
	○ ○ ○

KEY P: PROPHETIC B: BLESSING C: CURSE F: FIRST OCCURRENCE ?: QUESTION X: CROSS REFERENCE

DATE: **WEEK:**

B'REISHEET, GENESIS 6:9-11:32
NOACH, NOAH

Chet   Nun

HEADLINES

1.
2.
3.

CONFLICT/CHANGE	LESSON/APPLICATION

KEYWORDS	DEFINITIONS
1.	
2.	
3.	
4.	
5.	

PERSONAL TAKEAWAYS

1.
2.
3.

REFERENCE	NOTES	

KEY P: PROPHETIC B: BLESSING C: CURSE F: FIRST OCCURRENCE ?: QUESTION X: CROSS REFERENCE

DATE: **WEEK:**

B'REISHEET, GENESIS 12:1-17:27
LECH LECHA, GO FORTH!

	Khaf Sofit	Lamed		Khaf Sofit	Lamed

HEADLINES

1.
2.
3.

CONFLICT/CHANGE	LESSON/APPLICATION

KEYWORDS	DEFINITIONS
1.	
2.	
3.	
4.	
5.	

PERSONAL TAKEAWAYS

1.
2.
3.

REFERENCE	NOTES
	○ ○ ○
	○ ○ ○
	○ ○ ○
	○ ○ ○
	○ ○ ○
	○ ○ ○
	○ ○ ○
	○ ○ ○
	○ ○ ○
	○ ○ ○
	○ ○ ○
	○ ○ ○
	○ ○ ○
	○ ○ ○
	○ ○ ○
	○ ○ ○
	○ ○ ○
	○ ○ ○
	○ ○ ○
	○ ○ ○
	○ ○ ○
	○ ○ ○
	○ ○ ○
	○ ○ ○
	○ ○ ○
	○ ○ ○
	○ ○ ○
	○ ○ ○
	○ ○ ○
	○ ○ ○
	○ ○ ○

KEY   P: PROPHETIC   B: BLESSING   C: CURSE   F: FIRST OCCURRENCE   ?: QUESTION   X: CROSS REFERENCE

DATE: **WEEK:**

B'REISHEET, GENESIS 18:1-22:24
VAYERA, AND HE APPEARED

Aleph   Resh   Yod   Vav

HEADLINES
1.
2.
3.

CONFLICT/CHANGE	LESSON/APPLICATION

KEYWORDS	DEFINITIONS
1.	
2.	
3.	
4.	
5.	

PERSONAL TAKEAWAYS
1.
2.
3.

REFERENCE	NOTES				
	○ ○ ○				☐
	○ ○ ○				☐
	○ ○ ○				☐
	○ ○ ○				☐
	○ ○ ○				☐
	○ ○ ○				☐
	○ ○ ○				☐
	○ ○ ○				☐
	○ ○ ○				☐
	○ ○ ○				☐
	○ ○ ○				☐
	○ ○ ○				☐
	○ ○ ○				☐
	○ ○ ○				☐
	○ ○ ○				☐
	○ ○ ○				☐
	○ ○ ○				☐
	○ ○ ○				☐
	○ ○ ○				☐
	○ ○ ○				☐
	○ ○ ○				☐
	○ ○ ○				☐
	○ ○ ○				☐
	○ ○ ○				☐
	○ ○ ○				☐
	○ ○ ○				☐
	○ ○ ○				☐
	○ ○ ○				☐
	○ ○ ○				☐
	○ ○ ○				☐
	○ ○ ○				☐

KEY   P: PROPHETIC   B: BLESSING   C: CURSE   F: FIRST OCCURRENCE   ?: QUESTION   X: CROSS REFERENCE

DATE: WEK:

B'REISHEET, GENESIS 23:1-25:18
CHAYEI SARAH, LIFE OF SARAH

Hay   Resh   Sin   Yod   Yod   Chet

HEADLINES

1.
2.
3.

CONFLICT/CHANGE	LESSON/APPLICATION

KEYWORDS	DEFINITIONS
1.	
2.	
3.	
4.	
5.	

PERSONAL TAKEAWAYS

1.
2.
3.

REFERENCE	NOTES	
	○ ○ ○	☐
	○ ○ ○	☐
	○ ○ ○	☐
	○ ○ ○	☐
	○ ○ ○	☐
	○ ○ ○	☐
	○ ○ ○	☐
	○ ○ ○	☐
	○ ○ ○	☐
	○ ○ ○	☐
	○ ○ ○	☐
	○ ○ ○	☐
	○ ○ ○	☐
	○ ○ ○	☐
	○ ○ ○	☐
	○ ○ ○	☐
	○ ○ ○	☐
	○ ○ ○	☐
	○ ○ ○	☐
	○ ○ ○	☐
	○ ○ ○	☐
	○ ○ ○	☐
	○ ○ ○	☐
	○ ○ ○	☐
	○ ○ ○	☐
	○ ○ ○	☐
	○ ○ ○	☐
	○ ○ ○	☐
	○ ○ ○	☐
	○ ○ ○	☐
	○ ○ ○	☐
	○ ○ ○	☐

KEY P: PROPHETIC   B: BLESSING   C: CURSE   F: FIRST OCCURRENCE   ?: QUESTION   X: CROSS REFERENCE

DATE: **WEEK:**

B'REISHEET, GENESIS 25:19-28:9
TOLEDOT, GENERATIONS

Tav   Dalet   Lamed   Vav   Tav

HEADLINES

1.
2.
3.

CONFLICT/CHANGE	LESSON/APPLICATION

KEYWORDS	DEFINITIONS
1.	
2.	
3.	
4.	
5.	

PERSONAL TAKEAWAYS

1.
2.
3.

REFERENCE	NOTES
	○ ○ ○
	○ ○ ○
	○ ○ ○
	○ ○ ○
	○ ○ ○
	○ ○ ○
	○ ○ ○
	○ ○ ○
	○ ○ ○
	○ ○ ○
	○ ○ ○
	○ ○ ○
	○ ○ ○
	○ ○ ○
	○ ○ ○
	○ ○ ○
	○ ○ ○
	○ ○ ○
	○ ○ ○
	○ ○ ○
	○ ○ ○
	○ ○ ○
	○ ○ ○
	○ ○ ○
	○ ○ ○
	○ ○ ○
	○ ○ ○
	○ ○ ○
	○ ○ ○
	○ ○ ○
	○ ○ ○
	○ ○ ○

KEY P: PROPHETIC B: BLESSING C: CURSE F: FIRST OCCURRENCE ?: QUESTION X: CROSS REFERENCE

DATE: **WEEK:**

B'REISHEET, GENESIS 28:10-32:3
VAYETZE, AND HE WENT OUT

Aleph　Tzadi　Yod　Vav

HEADLINES
1.
2.
3.

CONFLICT/CHANGE	LESSON/APPLICATION

KEYWORDS	DEFINITIONS
1.	
2.	
3.	
4.	
5.	

PERSONAL TAKEAWAYS
1.
2.
3.

REFERENCE	NOTES
	○ ○ ○
	○ ○ ○
	○ ○ ○
	○ ○ ○
	○ ○ ○
	○ ○ ○
	○ ○ ○
	○ ○ ○
	○ ○ ○
	○ ○ ○
	○ ○ ○
	○ ○ ○
	○ ○ ○
	○ ○ ○
	○ ○ ○
	○ ○ ○
	○ ○ ○
	○ ○ ○
	○ ○ ○
	○ ○ ○
	○ ○ ○
	○ ○ ○
	○ ○ ○
	○ ○ ○
	○ ○ ○
	○ ○ ○
	○ ○ ○
	○ ○ ○
	○ ○ ○
	○ ○ ○
	○ ○ ○

KEY P: PROPHETIC B: BLESSING C: CURSE F: FIRST OCCURRENCE ?: QUESTION X: CROSS REFERENCE

DATE: **WEEK:**

B'REISHEET, GENESIS 32:4-36:43
VAYISHLACH, AND HE SENT

                                                          Chet   Lamed   Shin   Yod   Vav

HEADLINES

1.
2.
3.

CONFLICT/CHANGE	LESSON/APPLICATION

KEYWORDS	DEFINITIONS
1.	
2.	
3.	
4.	
5.	

PERSONAL TAKEAWAYS

1.
2.
3.

REFERENCE	NOTES
	○ ○ ○
	○ ○ ○
	○ ○ ○
	○ ○ ○
	○ ○ ○
	○ ○ ○
	○ ○ ○
	○ ○ ○
	○ ○ ○
	○ ○ ○
	○ ○ ○
	○ ○ ○
	○ ○ ○
	○ ○ ○
	○ ○ ○
	○ ○ ○
	○ ○ ○
	○ ○ ○
	○ ○ ○
	○ ○ ○
	○ ○ ○
	○ ○ ○
	○ ○ ○
	○ ○ ○
	○ ○ ○
	○ ○ ○
	○ ○ ○
	○ ○ ○
	○ ○ ○
	○ ○ ○
	○ ○ ○
	○ ○ ○

KEY   P: PROPHETIC   B: BLESSING   C: CURSE   F: FIRST OCCURRENCE   ?: QUESTION   X: CROSS REFERENCE

DATE: **WEEK:**

B'REISHEET, GENESIS 37:1-40:23
VAYESHEV, AND HE SETTLED

Vet　　Shin　　Yod　　Vav

HEADLINES

1.
2.
3.

CONFLICT/CHANGE	LESSON/APPLICATION

KEYWORDS	DEFINITIONS
1.	
2.	
3.	
4.	
5.	

PERSONAL TAKEAWAYS

1.
2.
3.

REFERENCE	NOTES
	○ ○ ○
	○ ○ ○
	○ ○ ○
	○ ○ ○
	○ ○ ○
	○ ○ ○
	○ ○ ○
	○ ○ ○
	○ ○ ○
	○ ○ ○
	○ ○ ○
	○ ○ ○
	○ ○ ○
	○ ○ ○
	○ ○ ○
	○ ○ ○
	○ ○ ○
	○ ○ ○
	○ ○ ○
	○ ○ ○
	○ ○ ○
	○ ○ ○
	○ ○ ○
	○ ○ ○
	○ ○ ○
	○ ○ ○
	○ ○ ○
	○ ○ ○
	○ ○ ○
	○ ○ ○
	○ ○ ○
	○ ○ ○

KEY   P: PROPHETIC   B: BLESSING   C: CURSE   F: FIRST OCCURRENCE   ?: QUESTION   X: CROSS REFERENCE

DATE: WEEK:

B'REISHEET, GENESIS 41:1-44:17
MIKETZ, AT THE END OF

Tzadi Sofit   Qof   Mem

HEADLINES

1.
2.
3.

CONFLICT/CHANGE	LESSON/APPLICATION

KEYWORDS	DEFINITIONS
1.	
2.	
3.	
4.	
5.	

PERSONAL TAKEAWAYS

1.
2.
3.

REFERENCE	NOTES

KEY   P: PROPHETIC   B: BLESSING   C: CURSE   F: FIRST OCCURRENCE   ?: QUESTION   X: CROSS REFERENCE

DATE: WEEK:

B'REISHEET, GENESIS 44:18-47:27
VAYIGASH, AND HE DREW NEAR

Shin   Gimel   Yod   Vav

HEADLINES
1.
2.
3.

CONFLICT/CHANGE	LESSON/APPLICATION

KEYWORDS	DEFINITIONS
1.	
2.	
3.	
4.	
5.	

PERSONAL TAKEAWAYS
1.
2.
3.

REFERENCE	NOTES
	○ ○ ○
	○ ○ ○
	○ ○ ○
	○ ○ ○
	○ ○ ○
	○ ○ ○
	○ ○ ○
	○ ○ ○
	○ ○ ○
	○ ○ ○
	○ ○ ○
	○ ○ ○
	○ ○ ○
	○ ○ ○
	○ ○ ○
	○ ○ ○
	○ ○ ○
	○ ○ ○
	○ ○ ○
	○ ○ ○
	○ ○ ○
	○ ○ ○
	○ ○ ○
	○ ○ ○
	○ ○ ○
	○ ○ ○
	○ ○ ○
	○ ○ ○
	○ ○ ○
	○ ○ ○

KEY   P: PROPHETIC   B: BLESSING   C: CURSE   F: FIRST OCCURRENCE   ?: QUESTION   X: CROSS REFERENCE

DATE: WEEK:

B'REISHEET, GENESIS 47:28-50:26
VAYECHI, AND HE LIVED

Yod   Chet   Yod   Vav

HEADLINES

1.
2.
3.

CONFLICT/CHANGE	LESSON/APPLICATION

KEYWORDS	DEFINITIONS
1.	
2.	
3.	
4.	
5.	

PERSONAL TAKEAWAYS

1.
2.
3.

REFERENCE	NOTES
	○ ○ ○
	○ ○ ○
	○ ○ ○
	○ ○ ○
	○ ○ ○
	○ ○ ○
	○ ○ ○
	○ ○ ○
	○ ○ ○
	○ ○ ○
	○ ○ ○
	○ ○ ○
	○ ○ ○
	○ ○ ○
	○ ○ ○
	○ ○ ○
	○ ○ ○
	○ ○ ○
	○ ○ ○
	○ ○ ○
	○ ○ ○
	○ ○ ○
	○ ○ ○
	○ ○ ○
	○ ○ ○
	○ ○ ○
	○ ○ ○
	○ ○ ○
	○ ○ ○
	○ ○ ○
	○ ○ ○

KEY P: PROPHETIC B: BLESSING C: CURSE F: FIRST OCCURRENCE ?: QUESTION X: CROSS REFERENCE

DATE: **WEek:**

SHEMOT, EXODUS 1:1-6:1
SHEMOT, NAMES

Tav   Vav   Mem   Shin

HEADLINES
1.
2.
3.

CONFLICT/CHANGE	LESSON/APPLICATION

KEYWORDS	DEFINITIONS
1.	
2.	
3.	
4.	
5.	

PERSONAL TAKEAWAYS
1.
2.
3.

REFERENCE	NOTES		
	○ ○ ○		
	○ ○ ○		
	○ ○ ○		
	○ ○ ○		
	○ ○ ○		
	○ ○ ○		
	○ ○ ○		
	○ ○ ○		
	○ ○ ○		
	○ ○ ○		
	○ ○ ○		
	○ ○ ○		
	○ ○ ○		
	○ ○ ○		
	○ ○ ○		
	○ ○ ○		
	○ ○ ○		
	○ ○ ○		
	○ ○ ○		
	○ ○ ○		
	○ ○ ○		
	○ ○ ○		
	○ ○ ○		
	○ ○ ○		
	○ ○ ○		
	○ ○ ○		
	○ ○ ○		
	○ ○ ○		
	○ ○ ○		
	○ ○ ○		
	○ ○ ○		
	○ ○ ○		

KEY   P: PROPHETIC   B: BLESSING   C: CURSE   F: FIRST OCCURRENCE   ?: QUESTION   X: CROSS REFERENCE

DATE:	WEEK:

SHEMOT, EXODUS 6:2-9:35
VA'ERA, APPEARED

Aleph   Resh   Aleph   Vav

HEADLINES

1.
2.
3.

CONFLICT/CHANGE	LESSON/APPLICATION

KEYWORDS	DEFINITIONS
1.	
2.	
3.	
4.	
5.	

PERSONAL TAKEAWAYS

1.
2.
3.

REFERENCE	NOTES

KEY P: PROPHETIC   B: BLESSING   C: CURSE   F: FIRST OCCURRENCE   ?: QUESTION   X: CROSS REFERENCE

DATE: **WEEK:**

SHEMOT, EXODUS 10:1-13:16
BO, GO

Aleph Bet

HEADLINES

1.
2.
3.

CONFLICT/CHANGE	LESSON/APPLICATION

KEYWORDS	DEFINITIONS
1.	
2.	
3.	
4.	
5.	

PERSONAL TAKEAWAYS

1.
2.
3.

REFERENCE	NOTES
	○ ○ ○
	○ ○ ○
	○ ○ ○
	○ ○ ○
	○ ○ ○
	○ ○ ○
	○ ○ ○
	○ ○ ○
	○ ○ ○
	○ ○ ○
	○ ○ ○
	○ ○ ○
	○ ○ ○
	○ ○ ○
	○ ○ ○
	○ ○ ○
	○ ○ ○
	○ ○ ○
	○ ○ ○
	○ ○ ○
	○ ○ ○
	○ ○ ○
	○ ○ ○
	○ ○ ○
	○ ○ ○
	○ ○ ○
	○ ○ ○
	○ ○ ○
	○ ○ ○
	○ ○ ○
	○ ○ ○
	○ ○ ○

KEY **P:** PROPHETIC **B:** BLESSING **C:** CURSE **F:** FIRST OCCURRENCE **?:** QUESTION **X:** CROSS REFERENCE

DATE: **WEEK:**

SHEMOT, EXODUS 13:17-17:16
BESHALACH, WHEN HE SENT OUT

Chet Lamed Shin Bet

HEADLINES

1.
2.
3.

CONFLICT/CHANGE	LESSON/APPLICATION

KEYWORDS	DEFINITIONS
1.	
2.	
3.	
4.	
5.	

PERSONAL TAKEAWAYS

1.
2.
3.

REFERENCE	NOTES
	○ ○ ○
	○ ○ ○
	○ ○ ○
	○ ○ ○
	○ ○ ○
	○ ○ ○
	○ ○ ○
	○ ○ ○
	○ ○ ○
	○ ○ ○
	○ ○ ○
	○ ○ ○
	○ ○ ○
	○ ○ ○
	○ ○ ○
	○ ○ ○
	○ ○ ○
	○ ○ ○
	○ ○ ○
	○ ○ ○
	○ ○ ○
	○ ○ ○
	○ ○ ○
	○ ○ ○
	○ ○ ○
	○ ○ ○
	○ ○ ○
	○ ○ ○
	○ ○ ○
	○ ○ ○
	○ ○ ○

KEY   P: PROPHETIC   B: BLESSING   C: CURSE   F: FIRST OCCURRENCE   ?: QUESTION   X: CROSS REFERENCE

DATE: WEEK:

SHEMOT, EXODUS 18:1-20:23
YITRO, JETHRO

                                                                                            Vav   Resh   Tav   Yod

HEADLINES

1.
2.
3.

CONFLICT/CHANGE	LESSON/APPLICATION

KEYWORDS	DEFINITIONS
1.	
2.	
3.	
4.	
5.	

PERSONAL TAKEAWAYS

1.
2.
3.

REFERENCE	NOTES			
	○	○	○	☐
	○	○	○	☐
	○	○	○	☐
	○	○	○	☐
	○	○	○	☐
	○	○	○	☐
	○	○	○	☐
	○	○	○	☐
	○	○	○	☐
	○	○	○	☐
	○	○	○	☐
	○	○	○	☐
	○	○	○	☐
	○	○	○	☐
	○	○	○	☐
	○	○	○	☐
	○	○	○	☐
	○	○	○	☐
	○	○	○	☐
	○	○	○	☐
	○	○	○	☐
	○	○	○	☐
	○	○	○	☐
	○	○	○	☐
	○	○	○	☐
	○	○	○	☐
	○	○	○	☐
	○	○	○	☐
	○	○	○	☐
	○	○	○	☐
	○	○	○	☐
	○	○	○	☐

KEY P: PROPHETIC B: BLESSING C: CURSE F: FIRST OCCURRENCE ?: QUESTION X: CROSS REFERENCE

DATE: **WEEK:**

SHEMOT, EXODUS 21:1-24:18
MISHPATIM, LAWS

| | Mem Sofit | Yod | Tet | Pey | Shin | Mem |

HEADLINES

1.
2.
3.

CONFLICT/CHANGE	LESSON/APPLICATION

KEYWORDS	DEFINITIONS
1.	
2.	
3.	
4.	
5.	

PERSONAL TAKEAWAYS

1.
2.
3.

REFERENCE	NOTES
	○ ○ ○
	○ ○ ○
	○ ○ ○
	○ ○ ○
	○ ○ ○
	○ ○ ○
	○ ○ ○
	○ ○ ○
	○ ○ ○
	○ ○ ○
	○ ○ ○
	○ ○ ○
	○ ○ ○
	○ ○ ○
	○ ○ ○
	○ ○ ○
	○ ○ ○
	○ ○ ○
	○ ○ ○
	○ ○ ○
	○ ○ ○
	○ ○ ○
	○ ○ ○
	○ ○ ○
	○ ○ ○
	○ ○ ○
	○ ○ ○
	○ ○ ○
	○ ○ ○
	○ ○ ○
	○ ○ ○
	○ ○ ○

KEY **P: PROPHETIC   B: BLESSING   C: CURSE   F: FIRST OCCURRENCE   ?: QUESTION   X: CROSS REFERENCE**

DATE: **WEEK:**

SHEMOT, EXODUS 25:1-27:19
TERUMAH, OFFERING

Hay   Mem   Vav   Resh   Tav

HEADLINES

1.
2.
3.

CONFLICT/CHANGE	LESSON/APPLICATION

KEYWORDS	DEFINITIONS
1.	
2.	
3.	
4.	
5.	

PERSONAL TAKEAWAYS

1.
2.
3.

REFERENCE	NOTES
	○ ○ ○
	○ ○ ○
	○ ○ ○
	○ ○ ○
	○ ○ ○
	○ ○ ○
	○ ○ ○
	○ ○ ○
	○ ○ ○
	○ ○ ○
	○ ○ ○
	○ ○ ○
	○ ○ ○
	○ ○ ○
	○ ○ ○
	○ ○ ○
	○ ○ ○
	○ ○ ○
	○ ○ ○
	○ ○ ○
	○ ○ ○
	○ ○ ○
	○ ○ ○
	○ ○ ○
	○ ○ ○
	○ ○ ○
	○ ○ ○
	○ ○ ○
	○ ○ ○
	○ ○ ○
	○ ○ ○
	○ ○ ○

KEY P: PROPHETIC   B: BLESSING   C: CURSE   F: FIRST OCCURRENCE   ?: QUESTION   X: CROSS REFERENCE

DATE: WEEK:

SHEMOT, EXODUS 27:20-30:10
TETZAVEH, YOU SHALL COMMAND

                                                              Hay   Vav   Tzadi   Tav

HEADLINES
1.
2.
3.

CONFLICT/CHANGE	LESSON/APPLICATION

KEYWORDS	DEFINITIONS
1.	
2.	
3.	
4.	
5.	

PERSONAL TAKEAWAYS
1.
2.
3.

REFERENCE	NOTES

KEY P: PROPHETIC B: BLESSING C: CURSE F: FIRST OCCURRENCE ?: QUESTION X: CROSS REFERENCE

DATE: **WEEK:**

SHEMOT, EXODUS 30:11-34:35
KI TISA, WHEN YOU ELEVATE

Aleph   Sin   Tav   Vav   Yod   Khaf

HEADLINES
1.
2.
3.

CONFLICT/CHANGE	LESSON/APPLICATION

KEYWORDS	DEFINITIONS
1.	
2.	
3.	
4.	
5.	

PERSONAL TAKEAWAYS
1.
2.
3.

REFERENCE	NOTES	
	○ ○ ○	☐
	○ ○ ○	☐
	○ ○ ○	☐
	○ ○ ○	☐
	○ ○ ○	☐
	○ ○ ○	☐
	○ ○ ○	☐
	○ ○ ○	☐
	○ ○ ○	☐
	○ ○ ○	☐
	○ ○ ○	☐
	○ ○ ○	☐
	○ ○ ○	☐
	○ ○ ○	☐
	○ ○ ○	☐
	○ ○ ○	☐
	○ ○ ○	☐
	○ ○ ○	☐
	○ ○ ○	☐
	○ ○ ○	☐
	○ ○ ○	☐
	○ ○ ○	☐
	○ ○ ○	☐
	○ ○ ○	☐
	○ ○ ○	☐
	○ ○ ○	☐
	○ ○ ○	☐
	○ ○ ○	☐
	○ ○ ○	☐
	○ ○ ○	☐
	○ ○ ○	☐
	○ ○ ○	☐

KEY   **P: PROPHETIC**   **B: BLESSING**   **C: CURSE**   **F: FIRST OCCURRENCE**   **?: QUESTION**   **X: CROSS REFERENCE**

DATE: **WEEK:**

SHEMOT, EXODUS 35:1-38:20 (OFTEN COMBINED WITH PEKUDEI)
VAYAKHEL, AND HE ASSEMBLED

Lamed   Hay   Qof   Yod   Vav

HEADLINES

1.
2.
3.

CONFLICT/CHANGE	LESSON/APPLICATION

KEYWORDS	DEFINITIONS
1.	
2.	
3.	
4.	
5.	

PERSONAL TAKEAWAYS

1.
2.
3.

REFERENCE	NOTES
	○ ○ ○
	○ ○ ○
	○ ○ ○
	○ ○ ○
	○ ○ ○
	○ ○ ○
	○ ○ ○
	○ ○ ○
	○ ○ ○
	○ ○ ○
	○ ○ ○
	○ ○ ○
	○ ○ ○
	○ ○ ○
	○ ○ ○
	○ ○ ○
	○ ○ ○
	○ ○ ○
	○ ○ ○
	○ ○ ○
	○ ○ ○
	○ ○ ○
	○ ○ ○
	○ ○ ○
	○ ○ ○
	○ ○ ○
	○ ○ ○
	○ ○ ○
	○ ○ ○
	○ ○ ○
	○ ○ ○
	○ ○ ○

KEY   **P:** PROPHETIC   **B:** BLESSING   **C:** CURSE   **F:** FIRST OCCURRENCE   **?:** QUESTION   **X:** CROSS REFERENCE

DATE: **WEEK:**

SHEMOT, EXODUS 38:21-40:38 (OFTEN COMBINED WITH VAYAKHEL)
PEKUDEI, ACCOUNTINGS

Yod   Dalet   Vav   Qof   Pey

HEADLINES
1.
2.
3.

CONFLICT/CHANGE	LESSON/APPLICATION

KEYWORDS	DEFINITIONS
1.	
2.	
3.	
4.	
5.	

PERSONAL TAKEAWAYS
1.
2.
3.

REFERENCE	NOTES	
	○ ○ ○	☐
	○ ○ ○	☐
	○ ○ ○	☐
	○ ○ ○	☐
	○ ○ ○	☐
	○ ○ ○	☐
	○ ○ ○	☐
	○ ○ ○	☐
	○ ○ ○	☐
	○ ○ ○	☐
	○ ○ ○	☐
	○ ○ ○	☐
	○ ○ ○	☐
	○ ○ ○	☐
	○ ○ ○	☐
	○ ○ ○	☐
	○ ○ ○	☐
	○ ○ ○	☐
	○ ○ ○	☐
	○ ○ ○	☐
	○ ○ ○	☐
	○ ○ ○	☐
	○ ○ ○	☐
	○ ○ ○	☐
	○ ○ ○	☐
	○ ○ ○	☐
	○ ○ ○	☐
	○ ○ ○	☐
	○ ○ ○	☐
	○ ○ ○	☐
	○ ○ ○	☐

KEY P: PROPHETIC B: BLESSING C: CURSE F: FIRST OCCURRENCE ?: QUESTION X: CROSS REFERENCE

DATE: **WEEK:**

VAYIKRA, LEVITICUS 1:1-5:26
VAYIKRA, AND HE CALLED

Aleph   Resh   Qof   Yod   Vav

HEADLINES

1.
2.
3.

CONFLICT/CHANGE	LESSON/APPLICATION

KEYWORDS	DEFINITIONS
1.	
2.	
3.	
4.	
5.	

PERSONAL TAKEAWAYS

1.
2.
3.

REFERENCE	NOTES
	○ ○ ○
	○ ○ ○
	○ ○ ○
	○ ○ ○
	○ ○ ○
	○ ○ ○
	○ ○ ○
	○ ○ ○
	○ ○ ○
	○ ○ ○
	○ ○ ○
	○ ○ ○
	○ ○ ○
	○ ○ ○
	○ ○ ○
	○ ○ ○
	○ ○ ○
	○ ○ ○
	○ ○ ○
	○ ○ ○
	○ ○ ○
	○ ○ ○
	○ ○ ○
	○ ○ ○
	○ ○ ○
	○ ○ ○
	○ ○ ○
	○ ○ ○
	○ ○ ○
	○ ○ ○
	○ ○ ○
	○ ○ ○

KEY   P: PROPHETIC   B: BLESSING   C: CURSE   F: FIRST OCCURRENCE   ?: QUESTION   X: CROSS REFERENCE

DATE: **WEEK:**

VAYKIRA, LEVITICUS 6:1-8:36
TZAV, COMMAND

Vav   Tzadi

HEADLINES

1.
2.
3.

CONFLICT/CHANGE	LESSON/APPLICATION

KEYWORDS	DEFINITIONS
1.	
2.	
3.	
4.	
5.	

PERSONAL TAKEAWAYS

1.
2.
3.

REFERENCE	NOTES				
	○	○	○		☐
	○	○	○		☐
	○	○	○		☐
	○	○	○		☐
	○	○	○		☐
	○	○	○		☐
	○	○	○		☐
	○	○	○		☐
	○	○	○		☐
	○	○	○		☐
	○	○	○		☐
	○	○	○		☐
	○	○	○		☐
	○	○	○		☐
	○	○	○		☐
	○	○	○		☐
	○	○	○		☐
	○	○	○		☐
	○	○	○		☐
	○	○	○		☐
	○	○	○		☐
	○	○	○		☐
	○	○	○		☐
	○	○	○		☐
	○	○	○		☐
	○	○	○		☐
	○	○	○		☐
	○	○	○		☐
	○	○	○		☐
	○	○	○		☐
	○	○	○		☐
	○	○	○		☐

KEY P: PROPHETIC B: BLESSING C: CURSE F: FIRST OCCURRENCE ?: QUESTION X: CROSS REFERENCE

DATE: **WEEK:**

VAYKIRA, LEVITICUS 9:1-11:47
SHEMINI, EIGHTH

Yod Nun Yod Mem Shin

HEADLINES
1.
2.
3.

CONFLICT/CHANGE	LESSON/APPLICATION

KEYWORDS	DEFINITIONS
1.	
2.	
3.	
4.	
5.	

PERSONAL TAKEAWAYS
1.
2.
3.

REFERENCE	NOTES			
	○ ○ ○			☐

KEY P: PROPHETIC   B: BLESSING   C: CURSE   F: FIRST OCCURRENCE   ?: QUESTION   X: CROSS REFERENCE

DATE: **WEEK:**

VAYKIRA, LEVITICUS 12:1-13:59 (OFTEN COMBINED WITH METZORA)
TAZRIA, SHE BEARS SEED

Ayin   Yod   Resh   Zayin   Tav

HEADLINES

1.
2.
3.

CONFLICT/CHANGE	LESSON/APPLICATION

KEYWORDS	DEFINITIONS
1.	
2.	
3.	
4.	
5.	

PERSONAL TAKEAWAYS

1.
2.
3.

REFERENCE	NOTES	

KEY P: PROPHETIC B: BLESSING C: CURSE F: FIRST OCCURRENCE ?: QUESTION X: CROSS REFERENCE

DATE: **WEEK:**

VAYKIRA, LEVITICUS 14:1-15:33 (OFTEN COMBINED WITH TAZRIA)
METZORA, INFECTED ONE

Ayin   Resh   Tzadi   Mem

HEADLINES

1.
2.
3.

CONFLICT/CHANGE	LESSON/APPLICATION

KEYWORDS	DEFINITIONS
1.	
2.	
3.	
4.	
5.	

PERSONAL TAKEAWAYS

1.
2.
3.

REFERENCE	NOTES	
	○ ○ ○	☐
	○ ○ ○	☐
	○ ○ ○	☐
	○ ○ ○	☐
	○ ○ ○	☐
	○ ○ ○	☐
	○ ○ ○	☐
	○ ○ ○	☐
	○ ○ ○	☐
	○ ○ ○	☐
	○ ○ ○	☐
	○ ○ ○	☐
	○ ○ ○	☐
	○ ○ ○	☐
	○ ○ ○	☐
	○ ○ ○	☐
	○ ○ ○	☐
	○ ○ ○	☐
	○ ○ ○	☐
	○ ○ ○	☐
	○ ○ ○	☐
	○ ○ ○	☐
	○ ○ ○	☐
	○ ○ ○	☐
	○ ○ ○	☐
	○ ○ ○	☐
	○ ○ ○	☐
	○ ○ ○	☐
	○ ○ ○	☐
	○ ○ ○	☐
	○ ○ ○	☐
	○ ○ ○	☐

KEY P: PROPHETIC B: BLESSING C: CURSE F: FIRST OCCURRENCE ?: QUESTION X: CROSS REFERENCE

DATE: **WEEK:**

VAYKIRA, LEVITICUS 16:1-18:30 (OFTEN COMBINED WITH KEDOSHIM)
ACHAREI MOT, AFTER THE DEATH

Tav   Vav   Mem   Yod   Resh   Chet   Aleph

HEADLINES

1.
2.
3.

CONFLICT/CHANGE	LESSON/APPLICATION

KEYWORDS	DEFINITIONS
1.	
2.	
3.	
4.	
5.	

PERSONAL TAKEAWAYS

1.
2.
3.

REFERENCE	NOTES
	○ ○ ○
	○ ○ ○
	○ ○ ○
	○ ○ ○
	○ ○ ○
	○ ○ ○
	○ ○ ○
	○ ○ ○
	○ ○ ○
	○ ○ ○
	○ ○ ○
	○ ○ ○
	○ ○ ○
	○ ○ ○
	○ ○ ○
	○ ○ ○
	○ ○ ○
	○ ○ ○
	○ ○ ○
	○ ○ ○
	○ ○ ○
	○ ○ ○
	○ ○ ○
	○ ○ ○
	○ ○ ○
	○ ○ ○
	○ ○ ○
	○ ○ ○
	○ ○ ○
	○ ○ ○

KEY   **P: PROPHETIC**   **B: BLESSING**   **C: CURSE**   **F: FIRST OCCURRENCE**   **?: QUESTION**   **X: CROSS REFERENCE**

DATE: **WEEK:**

VAYKIRA, LEVITICUS 19:1-20:27 (OFTEN COMBINED WITH ACHAREI MOT)
KEDOSHIM, HOLY ONES

| | Mem Sofit | Yod | Shin | Dalet | Qof |

HEADLINES

1.
2.
3.

CONFLICT/CHANGE	LESSON/APPLICATION

KEYWORDS	DEFINITIONS
1.	
2.	
3.	
4.	
5.	

PERSONAL TAKEAWAYS

1.
2.
3.

REFERENCE	NOTES	

DATE: **WEEK:**

VAYKIRA, LEVITICUS 21:1-24:23
EMOR, SAY GENTLY

Resh　Mem　Alpeh

HEADLINES

1.
2.
3.

CONFLICT/CHANGE	LESSON/APPLICATION

KEYWORDS	DEFINITIONS
1.	
2.	
3.	
4.	
5.	

PERSONAL TAKEAWAYS

1.
2.
3.

REFERENCE	NOTES
	○ ○ ○
	○ ○ ○
	○ ○ ○
	○ ○ ○
	○ ○ ○
	○ ○ ○
	○ ○ ○
	○ ○ ○
	○ ○ ○
	○ ○ ○
	○ ○ ○
	○ ○ ○
	○ ○ ○
	○ ○ ○
	○ ○ ○
	○ ○ ○
	○ ○ ○
	○ ○ ○
	○ ○ ○
	○ ○ ○
	○ ○ ○
	○ ○ ○
	○ ○ ○
	○ ○ ○
	○ ○ ○
	○ ○ ○
	○ ○ ○
	○ ○ ○
	○ ○ ○
	○ ○ ○
	○ ○ ○
	○ ○ ○

KEY P: PROPHETIC B: BLESSING C: CURSE F: FIRST OCCURRENCE ?: QUESTION X: CROSS REFERENCE

DATE: **WEEK:**

VAYKIRA, LEVITICUS 25:1-26:2 (OFTEN COMBINED WITH BECHUKOTAI)
BEHAR, ON THE MOUNT

Resh Hay Bet

HEADLINES

1.
2.
3.

CONFLICT/CHANGE	LESSON/APPLICATION

KEYWORDS	DEFINITIONS
1.	
2.	
3.	
4.	
5.	

PERSONAL TAKEAWAYS

1.
2.
3.

REFERENCE	NOTES
	○ ○ ○
	○ ○ ○
	○ ○ ○
	○ ○ ○
	○ ○ ○
	○ ○ ○
	○ ○ ○
	○ ○ ○
	○ ○ ○
	○ ○ ○
	○ ○ ○
	○ ○ ○
	○ ○ ○
	○ ○ ○
	○ ○ ○
	○ ○ ○
	○ ○ ○
	○ ○ ○
	○ ○ ○
	○ ○ ○
	○ ○ ○
	○ ○ ○
	○ ○ ○
	○ ○ ○
	○ ○ ○
	○ ○ ○
	○ ○ ○
	○ ○ ○
	○ ○ ○
	○ ○ ○
	○ ○ ○
	○ ○ ○

KEY   P: PROPHETIC   B: BLESSING   C: CURSE   F: FIRST OCCURRENCE   ?: QUESTION   X: CROSS REFERENCE

DATE: **WEEK:**

VAYKIRA, LEVITICUS 26:3-27:34 (OFTEN COMBINED WITH BEHAR)
BECHUKOTAI, IN MY LAWS

                                                           Yod   Tav   Qof   Chet   Bet

HEADLINES

1.
2.
3.

CONFLICT/CHANGE	LESSON/APPLICATION

KEYWORDS	DEFINITIONS
1.	
2.	
3.	
4.	
5.	

PERSONAL TAKEAWAYS

1.
2.
3.

REFERENCE	NOTES	

KEY P: PROPHETIC B: BLESSING C: CURSE F: FIRST OCCURRENCE ?: QUESTION X: CROSS REFERENCE

DATE: WEEK:

BAMIDBAR, NUMBERS 1:1-4:20
BAMIDBAR, IN THE WILDERNESS

Resh   Bet   Dalet   Mem   Bet

HEADLINES

1.
2.
3.

CONFLICT/CHANGE	LESSON/APPLICATION

KEYWORDS	DEFINITIONS
1.	
2.	
3.	
4.	
5.	

PERSONAL TAKEAWAYS

1.
2.
3.

REFERENCE	NOTES

KEY P: PROPHETIC B: BLESSING C: CURSE F: FIRST OCCURRENCE ?: QUESTION X: CROSS REFERENCE

DATE: **WEEK:**

BAMIDBAR, NUMBERS 4:21-7:89
NASSO, ELEVATE

Aleph   Sin   Nun

HEADLINES

1.
2.
3.

CONFLICT/CHANGE	LESSON/APPLICATION

KEYWORDS	DEFINITIONS
1.	
2.	
3.	
4.	
5.	

PERSONAL TAKEAWAYS

1.
2.
3.

REFERENCE	NOTES

KEY   P: PROPHETIC   B: BLESSING   C: CURSE   F: FIRST OCCURRENCE   ?: QUESTION   X: CROSS REFERENCE

DATE: **WEEK:**

BAMIDBAR, NUMBERS 8:1-12:16
BEHA'ALOTCHA, IN YOUR UPLIFTING

	Khaf Sofit	Tav	Lamed	Ayin	Hay	Bet

HEADLINES

1.
2.
3.

CONFLICT/CHANGE	LESSON/APPLICATION

KEYWORDS	DEFINITIONS
1.	
2.	
3.	
4.	
5.	

PERSONAL TAKEAWAYS

1.
2.
3.

REFERENCE	NOTES	
	○ ○ ○	☐
	○ ○ ○	☐
	○ ○ ○	☐
	○ ○ ○	☐
	○ ○ ○	☐
	○ ○ ○	☐
	○ ○ ○	☐
	○ ○ ○	☐
	○ ○ ○	☐
	○ ○ ○	☐
	○ ○ ○	☐
	○ ○ ○	☐
	○ ○ ○	☐
	○ ○ ○	☐
	○ ○ ○	☐
	○ ○ ○	☐
	○ ○ ○	☐
	○ ○ ○	☐
	○ ○ ○	☐
	○ ○ ○	☐
	○ ○ ○	☐
	○ ○ ○	☐
	○ ○ ○	☐
	○ ○ ○	☐
	○ ○ ○	☐
	○ ○ ○	☐
	○ ○ ○	☐
	○ ○ ○	☐
	○ ○ ○	☐
	○ ○ ○	☐
	○ ○ ○	☐
	○ ○ ○	☐

KEY   **P: PROPHETIC**   **B: BLESSING**   **C: CURSE**   **F: FIRST OCCURRENCE**   **?: QUESTION**   **X: CROSS REFERENCE**

DATE: **WEEK:**

BAMIDBAR, NUMBERS 13:1-15:41
SHELACH, SEND FOR YOURSELF

Chet   Lamed   Shin

HEADLINES
1.
2.
3.

CONFLICT/CHANGE	LESSON/APPLICATION

KEYWORDS	DEFINITIONS
1.	
2.	
3.	
4.	
5.	

PERSONAL TAKEAWAYS
1.
2.
3.

REFERENCE	NOTES

KEY P: PROPHETIC B: BLESSING C: CURSE F: FIRST OCCURRENCE ?: QUESTION X: CROSS REFERENCE

DATE: **WEEK:**

BAMIDBAR, NUMBERS 16:1-18:32
KORACH, KORAH

                                                                             Chet   Resh   Qof

HEADLINES

1.
2.
3.

CONFLICT/CHANGE	LESSON/APPLICATION

KEYWORDS	DEFINITIONS
1.	
2.	
3.	
4.	
5.	

PERSONAL TAKEAWAYS

1.
2.
3.

REFERENCE	NOTES

KEY P: PROPHETIC   B: BLESSING   C: CURSE   F: FIRST OCCURRENCE   ?: QUESTION   X: CROSS REFERENCE

DATE: **WEEK:**

BAMIDBAR, NUMBERS 19:1-22:1 (OFTEN COMBINED WITH BALAK)
CHUKAT, LAW

Tav   Qof   Chet

HEADLINES

1.
2.
3.

CONFLICT/CHANGE	LESSON/APPLICATION

KEYWORDS	DEFINITIONS
1.	
2.	
3.	
4.	
5.	

PERSONAL TAKEAWAYS

1.
2.
3.

REFERENCE	NOTES

KEY   **P: PROPHETIC**   **B: BLESSING**   **C: CURSE**   **F: FIRST OCCURRENCE**   **?: QUESTION**   **X: CROSS REFERENCE**

DATE: WEEK:

BAMIDBAR, NUMBERS 22:2-25:9 (OFTEN COMBINED WITH CHUKAT)
BALAK, BALAK

Qof   Lamed   Bet

HEADLINES

1.
2.
3.

CONFLICT/CHANGE	LESSON/APPLICATION

KEYWORDS	DEFINITIONS
1.	
2.	
3.	
4.	
5.	

PERSONAL TAKEAWAYS

1.
2.
3.

REFERENCE	NOTES

KEY **P:** PROPHETIC **B:** BLESSING **C:** CURSE **F:** FIRST OCCURRENCE **?:** QUESTION **X:** CROSS REFERENCE

DATE: **WEEK:**

BAMIDBAR, NUMBERS 25:10-30:1
PINCHAS, PHINEHAS

Samekh Chet Nun Yod Pey

HEADLINES
1.
2.
3.

CONFLICT/CHANGE	LESSON/APPLICATION

KEYWORDS	DEFINITIONS
1.	
2.	
3.	
4.	
5.	

PERSONAL TAKEAWAYS
1.
2.
3.

REFERENCE	NOTES

KEY   P: PROPHETIC   B: BLESSING   C: CURSE   F: FIRST OCCURRENCE   ?: QUESTION   X: CROSS REFERENCE

DATE: WEEK:

BAMIDBAR, NUMBERS 30:2-32:42 (OFTEN COMBINED WITH MASSEI)
MATTOT, TRIBES

Tav   Vav   Tet   Mem

HEADLINES

1.
2.
3.

CONFLICT/CHANGE	LESSON/APPLICATION

KEYWORDS	DEFINITIONS
1.	
2.	
3.	
4.	
5.	

PERSONAL TAKEAWAYS

1.
2.
3.

REFERENCE	NOTES

KEY P: PROPHETIC B: BLESSING C: CURSE F: FIRST OCCURRENCE ?: QUESTION X: CROSS REFERENCE

DATE: WEEK:

BAMIDBAR, NUMBERS 33:1-36:13 (OFTEN COMBINED WITH MATTOT)
MASSEI, JOURNEYS OF

Yod   Ayin   Samekh   Mem

HEADLINES

1.
2.
3.

CONFLICT/CHANGE	LESSON/APPLICATION

KEYWORDS	DEFINITIONS
1.	
2.	
3.	
4.	
5.	

PERSONAL TAKEAWAYS

1.
2.
3.

REFERENCE	NOTES

KEY P: PROPHETIC B: BLESSING C: CURSE F: FIRST OCCURRENCE ?: QUESTION X: CROSS REFERENCE

DATE: **WEEK:**

DEVARIM, DEUTERONOMY 1:1-3:22
DEVARIM, WORDS

| | Mem Sofit | Yod | Resh | Vet | Dalet |

HEADLINES

1.
2.
3.

CONFLICT/CHANGE	LESSON/APPLICATION

KEYWORDS	DEFINITIONS
1.	
2.	
3.	
4.	
5.	

PERSONAL TAKEAWAYS

1.
2.
3.

REFERENCE	NOTES

KEY P: PROPHETIC B: BLESSING C: CURSE F: FIRST OCCURRENCE ?: QUESTION X: CROSS REFERENCE

DATE: **WEEK:**

DEVARIM, DEUTERONOMY 3:23-7:11
VA'ETCHANAN, PLEADED

		Nun Sofit	Nun	Chet	Tav	Aleph	Vav

HEADLINES

1.
2.
3.

CONFLICT/CHANGE	LESSON/APPLICATION

KEYWORDS	DEFINITIONS
1.	
2.	
3.	
4.	
5.	

PERSONAL TAKEAWAYS

1.
2.
3.

REFERENCE	NOTES

KEY P: PROPHETIC B: BLESSING C: CURSE F: FIRST OCCURRENCE ?: QUESTION X: CROSS REFERENCE

DATE: **WEEK:**

DEVARIM, DEUTERONOMY 7:12-11:25
EKEV, AS A RESULT

Vet   Qof   Ayin

HEADLINES

1.
2.
3.

CONFLICT/CHANGE	LESSON/APPLICATION

KEYWORDS	DEFINITIONS
1.	
2.	
3.	
4.	
5.	

PERSONAL TAKEAWAYS

1.
2.
3.

REFERENCE	NOTES				
	○	○	○		☐
	○	○	○		☐
	○	○	○		☐
	○	○	○		☐
	○	○	○		☐
	○	○	○		☐
	○	○	○		☐
	○	○	○		☐
	○	○	○		☐
	○	○	○		☐
	○	○	○		☐
	○	○	○		☐
	○	○	○		☐
	○	○	○		☐
	○	○	○		☐
	○	○	○		☐
	○	○	○		☐
	○	○	○		☐
	○	○	○		☐
	○	○	○		☐
	○	○	○		☐
	○	○	○		☐
	○	○	○		☐
	○	○	○		☐
	○	○	○		☐
	○	○	○		☐
	○	○	○		☐
	○	○	○		☐
	○	○	○		☐
	○	○	○		☐
	○	○	○		☐
	○	○	○		☐

KEY P: PROPHETIC B: BLESSING C: CURSE F: FIRST OCCURRENCE ?: QUESTION X: CROSS REFERENCE

DATE: **WEEK:**

DEVARIM, DEUTERONOMY 11:26-16:17
RE'EH, SEE

Hay   Aleph   Resh

HEADLINES

1.
2.
3.

CONFLICT/CHANGE	LESSON/APPLICATION

KEYWORDS	DEFINITIONS
1.	
2.	
3.	
4.	
5.	

PERSONAL TAKEAWAYS

1.
2.
3.

REFERENCE	NOTES				
	○	○	○		☐

KEY   **P:** PROPHETIC   **B:** BLESSING   **C:** CURSE   **F:** FIRST OCCURRENCE   **?:** QUESTION   **X:** CROSS REFERENCE

DATE: **WEEK:**

DEVARIM, DEUTERONOMY 16:18-21:9
SHOFTIM, JUDGES

| | Mem Sofit | Yod | Tet | Fey | Shin |

HEADLINES

1.
2.
3.

CONFLICT/CHANGE	LESSON/APPLICATION

KEYWORDS	DEFINITIONS
1.	
2.	
3.	
4.	
5.	

PERSONAL TAKEAWAYS

1.
2.
3.

REFERENCE	NOTES	

KEY   **P:** PROPHETIC   **B:** BLESSING   **C:** CURSE   **F:** FIRST OCCURRENCE   **?:** QUESTION   **X:** CROSS REFERENCE

DATE: **WEEK:**

DEVARIM, DEUTERONOMY 21:10-25:19
KI TETZE, WHEN YOU GO OUT

Aleph   Tzadi   Tav   Yod   Kaf

HEADLINES

1.
2.
3.

CONFLICT/CHANGE	LESSON/APPLICATION

KEYWORDS	DEFINITIONS
1.	
2.	
3.	
4.	
5.	

PERSONAL TAKEAWAYS

1.
2.
3.

REFERENCE	NOTES	
	○ ○ ○	☐
	○ ○ ○	☐
	○ ○ ○	☐
	○ ○ ○	☐
	○ ○ ○	☐
	○ ○ ○	☐
	○ ○ ○	☐
	○ ○ ○	☐
	○ ○ ○	☐
	○ ○ ○	☐
	○ ○ ○	☐
	○ ○ ○	☐
	○ ○ ○	☐
	○ ○ ○	☐
	○ ○ ○	☐
	○ ○ ○	☐
	○ ○ ○	☐
	○ ○ ○	☐
	○ ○ ○	☐
	○ ○ ○	☐
	○ ○ ○	☐
	○ ○ ○	☐
	○ ○ ○	☐
	○ ○ ○	☐
	○ ○ ○	☐
	○ ○ ○	☐
	○ ○ ○	☐
	○ ○ ○	☐
	○ ○ ○	☐
	○ ○ ○	☐
	○ ○ ○	☐
	○ ○ ○	☐
	○ ○ ○	☐

KEY   P: PROPHETIC   B: BLESSING   C: CURSE   F: FIRST OCCURRENCE   ?: QUESTION   X: CROSS REFERENCE

DATE: WEEK:

DEVARIM, DEUTERONOMY 26:1-29:8
KI TAVO, WHEN YOU ENTER IN

Alpeh　Vav　Vet　Tav　Yod　Kaf

HEADLINES

1.
2.
3.

CONFLICT/CHANGE	LESSON/APPLICATION

KEYWORDS	DEFINITIONS
1.	
2.	
3.	
4.	
5.	

PERSONAL TAKEAWAYS

1.
2.
3.

REFERENCE	NOTES

KEY   P: PROPHETIC   B: BLESSING   C: CURSE   F: FIRST OCCURRENCE   ?: QUESTION   X: CROSS REFERENCE

DATE: **WEEK:**

DEVARIM, DEUTERONOMY 29:9-30:20 (OFTEN COMBINED WITH VAYELECH)
NITZAVIM, STANDING (WITNESSING)

Mem Sofit | Yod | Vet | Tzadi | Nun

HEADLINES

1.
2.
3.

CONFLICT/CHANGE	LESSON/APPLICATION

KEYWORDS	DEFINITIONS
1.	
2.	
3.	
4.	
5.	

PERSONAL TAKEAWAYS

1.
2.
3.

REFERENCE	NOTES	
	○ ○ ○	☐
	○ ○ ○	☐
	○ ○ ○	☐
	○ ○ ○	☐
	○ ○ ○	☐
	○ ○ ○	☐
	○ ○ ○	☐
	○ ○ ○	☐
	○ ○ ○	☐
	○ ○ ○	☐
	○ ○ ○	☐
	○ ○ ○	☐
	○ ○ ○	☐
	○ ○ ○	☐
	○ ○ ○	☐
	○ ○ ○	☐
	○ ○ ○	☐
	○ ○ ○	☐
	○ ○ ○	☐
	○ ○ ○	☐
	○ ○ ○	☐
	○ ○ ○	☐
	○ ○ ○	☐
	○ ○ ○	☐
	○ ○ ○	☐
	○ ○ ○	☐
	○ ○ ○	☐
	○ ○ ○	☐
	○ ○ ○	☐
	○ ○ ○	☐
	○ ○ ○	☐
	○ ○ ○	☐

KEY P: PROPHETIC B: BLESSING C: CURSE F: FIRST OCCURRENCE ?: QUESTION X: CROSS REFERENCE

DATE: **WEEK:**

DEVARIM, DEUTERONOMY 31:1-31:30 (OFTEN COMBINED WITH NITZAVIM)
VAYELECH, AND HE WENT

Khaf Sofit   Lamed   Yod   Vav

HEADLINES

1.
2.
3.

CONFLICT/CHANGE	LESSON/APPLICATION

KEYWORDS	DEFINITIONS
1.	
2.	
3.	
4.	
5.	

PERSONAL TAKEAWAYS

1.
2.
3.

REFERENCE	NOTES

KEY P: PROPHETIC   B: BLESSING   C: CURSE   F: FIRST OCCURRENCE   ?: QUESTION   X: CROSS REFERENCE

DATE: **WEEK:**

DEVARIM, DEUTERONOMY 32:1-32:52
HA'AZINU, LISTEN

                                               Vav   Nun   Yod   Zayin   Alpeh   Hay

HEADLINES

1.
2.
3.

CONFLICT/CHANGE	LESSON/APPLICATION

KEYWORDS	DEFINITIONS
1.	
2.	
3.	
4.	
5.	

PERSONAL TAKEAWAYS

1.
2.
3.

REFERENCE	NOTES	
	○ ○ ○	☐
	○ ○ ○	☐
	○ ○ ○	☐
	○ ○ ○	☐
	○ ○ ○	☐
	○ ○ ○	☐
	○ ○ ○	☐
	○ ○ ○	☐
	○ ○ ○	☐
	○ ○ ○	☐
	○ ○ ○	☐
	○ ○ ○	☐
	○ ○ ○	☐
	○ ○ ○	☐
	○ ○ ○	☐
	○ ○ ○	☐
	○ ○ ○	☐
	○ ○ ○	☐
	○ ○ ○	☐
	○ ○ ○	☐
	○ ○ ○	☐
	○ ○ ○	☐
	○ ○ ○	☐
	○ ○ ○	☐
	○ ○ ○	☐
	○ ○ ○	☐
	○ ○ ○	☐
	○ ○ ○	☐
	○ ○ ○	☐
	○ ○ ○	☐
	○ ○ ○	☐
	○ ○ ○	☐

KEY P: PROPHETIC B: BLESSING C: CURSE F: FIRST OCCURRENCE ?: QUESTION X: CROSS REFERENCE

DATE: **WEEK:**

DEVARIM, DEUTERONOMY 33:1-34:12
VEZOT HABRACHA, AND THIS IS THE BLESSING

Hay　　Kaf　　Resh　　Bet　　Hay　　　　Tav　　Aleph　　Zayin　　Vav

HEADLINES

1.
2.
3.

CONFLICT/CHANGE	LESSON/APPLICATION

KEYWORDS	DEFINITIONS
1.	
2.	
3.	
4.	
5.	

PERSONAL TAKEAWAYS

1.
2.
3.

REFERENCE	NOTES				
	○	○	○		☐
	○	○	○		☐
	○	○	○		☐
	○	○	○		☐
	○	○	○		☐
	○	○	○		☐
	○	○	○		☐
	○	○	○		☐
	○	○	○		☐
	○	○	○		☐
	○	○	○		☐
	○	○	○		☐
	○	○	○		☐
	○	○	○		☐
	○	○	○		☐
	○	○	○		☐
	○	○	○		☐
	○	○	○		☐
	○	○	○		☐
	○	○	○		☐
	○	○	○		☐
	○	○	○		☐
	○	○	○		☐
	○	○	○		☐
	○	○	○		☐
	○	○	○		☐
	○	○	○		☐
	○	○	○		☐
	○	○	○		☐
	○	○	○		☐
	○	○	○		☐

KEY P: PROPHETIC B: BLESSING C: CURSE F: FIRST OCCURRENCE ?: QUESTION X: CROSS REFERENCE

DATE: **WEEK:**

FINAL REVIEW

CENTRAL THEMES & MESSAGES

FUTURE STUDY & CONTEMPLATION

STUDY CONCLUSION

HEBREW REFERENCE GUIDE

* Also used to hold a vowel marking indicating either an "O" (וֹ) or "OO" (וּ) sound.

Use this guide to the Hebrew alphabet to gain further understanding of the original meaning of each word. Each letter is shown in both its modern and Paleo styles. Hebrew letters hold both a numerical value and a traditional meaning. The meaning of a letter is generally derived from the Paleo imagery, related hieroglyphs from that era, and/or the similarity between a Hebrew word and the pronounced sound of the letter's name. Examples include Lamed appearing like a shepherd's staff and Yod being phonetically similar to the Hebrew word for "hand," which is pronounced "yad."

Hebrew is read from right to left. Certain letters take on the "sofit" (final) form when used as the last letter in a word. In its original form, Hebrew did not contain vowel marks.

www.ingramcontent.com/pod-product-compliance
Lightning Source LLC
Chambersburg PA
CBHW030636150426

42811CB00077B/2178/J